Academic
Learning
Series

Networking
Essentials Plus
Third Edition

Lab Manual

PUBLISHED BY
Microsoft Press
A Division of Microsoft Corporation
One Microsoft Way
Redmond, Washington 98052-6399

Copyright © 2000 by Microsoft Corporation

Library of Congress Cataloging-in-Publication Data
Academic Learning Series Networking Essentials Plus -- 3rd ed.
       p. cm. -- (Academic learning series)
   Includes index.
   ISBN 1-57231-902-X
   ISBN 0-7356-0912-8 (Academic Learning Series)
   1. Computer networks. I. Series.

  TK5105.5 N4669   2000
  004.6--dc21   99-054166

Printed and bound in the United States of America.

1 2 3 4 5 6 7 8 9   WCWC   5 4 3 2 1 0

Distributed in Canada by Penguin Books Canada Limited.

A CIP catalogue record for this book is available from the British Library.

Microsoft Press books are available through booksellers and distributors worldwide. For further information about international editions, contact your local Microsoft Corporation office or contact Microsoft Press International directly at fax (425) 936-7329. Visit our Web site at mspress.microsoft.com.

BackOffice, Microsoft, Microsoft Press, MS-DOS, MSN, Visual Basic, Windows, the Windows logo, and Windows NT are either registered trademarks or trademarks of Microsoft Corporation. Other product and company names mentioned herein may be the trademarks of their respective owners.

Acquisitions Editor: William Setten
Project Editor: Maureen Phillips
Technical Editor: Steve Perry

Part No. 097-0002873

Introduction to Lab Exercises

Included with the Networking Essentials text are hands-on lab exercises designed to give you practical experience using Microsoft Windows 2000 Server. This experience is an essential part of your training because it is difficult to truly understand and use the operating system and its features without having first had the opportunity to explore the menus, options, and responses. The tasks included in these exercises provide an opportunity for you to test the concepts presented in the text, to use Microsoft Windows 2000 utilities and tools, and to explore the structure of the Microsoft Windows 2000 operating system.

The lab exercises are best used in a classroom setting, though some exercises can be completed individually. The exercises presume a classroom network set up as a Windows 2000 domain with shared resources. A Lab Setup Guide is provided on the instructor CD for use in setting up the classroom.

Keep in mind that the lab exercises do not precisely mirror the text's practice activities. Domain names, user names, IP addresses, shared resources, and other specific references in the lab exercises may be somewhat different from similar references in the ALS text or from those used in setting up the classroom network.

Local constraints must be observed to ensure proper network operations. Since it is not possible to predict each institution's local networking requirements, your instructor will explain any differences.

The old saying "The way to get to Carnegie Hall is to practice, practice, practice" is equally true of the pursuit of competence for the CompTIA Network+ certification exam. One of the best ways to become confident in the use of Microsoft Windows 2000 is to complete each of the assigned lab exercises at least once, as well as completing the practice tasks included in the text.

Lab 1: Logging On to the Domain

Objectives

After completing this lab, you will be able to:

- Log on to the Corpx domain.

Estimated time to complete this lab: 10 minutes

Exercise 1
Logging On to the Corp*x* Domain

In this exercise, you will learn how to log on to the Corp*x* domain so that you can access resources on the domain controller. You have been provided with a student account, named Student*x*, to use to log on to the domain.

▶ **To log on to the Corp*x* domain**

1. Start your Windows 2000 Server.

2. When the **Welcome to Windows** dialog box appears, press CTRL+ALT+DELETE to display the **Log On to Windows** dialog box.

3. In **User name**, type **Student*x***.

4. In **Password**, type **password**.

5. The **Log on to** field should appear below the **password** field. If it doesn't, click **Options**. Make sure **CORP*x*** appears in the **Log on to** field. If it isn't there already, select it from the drop-down list.

You should now be logged on to the domain as the Student*x* user. If this does not work, repeat the steps above or ask your instructor for help. If you are having difficulty, remember to check the spelling of the user name. Although it is not case-sensitive, the specific characters in your user name must be typed correctly, including the numerical digit(s) at the end of the name.

Lab 2: Using System Tools to View System Information

Objectives

After completing this lab, you will be able to:

- Determine the hardware and software resources installed on a Windows 2000 system.
- Create a System Information file.

Exercise 1
Using Windows System Tools to View System Information

In this exercise, you will use MSInfo32 to view system information for your Windows 2000 Server.

▶ **To view system information**

1. Log on to the domain as Student*x*.

2. Click **Start**, point to **Programs**, point to **Administrative Tools**, and then click **Computer Management**. The **Computer Management** console will appear. The **System Tools** node should already be expanded, but if it isn't, double-click **System Tools**. Double-click **System Information**. As an alternative, you can click **Start**, click **Run**, and then type **MSInfo32**.

3. Locate the following information by reviewing the contents of the **System Information** containers (folders). For each item requested in the table below, record the name of the container where you found the item and the value of the item.

   Answers recorded in the table will vary from student to student.

Item	Container	Value
OS Name		
Version		
Build		
Windows Directory		
Display Adapter Type		
Network Adapter Name		
Processor		

4. Locate the following information, and then record the value of each item requested in the table below.

   Answers recorded in the table will vary from student to student.

Item	Value
Total Physical Memory	
Available Physical Memory	
Page File Space	
Available Virtual Memory	

Exercise 2
Saving a Windows 2000 System Information file

In this exercise, you will save a Windows 2000 System Information file for your computer, and then view the file.

▶ **To create a Windows 2000 System Information file**

1. Open the **Computer Management** or **System Information** console as you did in Exercise 1.

2. Right-click **System Information**.

3. Click **Save As System InformationFile**.

4. Save the file as C:\My Documents\System Info.nfo.

▶ **To view your Windows 2000 System Information file**

1. Click **Start**, point to **Documents**, and then click **My Documents**.

2. Double-click **System Info.nfo** to view the file contents.

3. Right-click **System Information**, and then click **Find**. In the Windows 2000 System Information file you just created, locate the following information.

Item	Value
PROCESSOR_ARCHITECTURE	
PROCESSOR_LEVEL	
PROCESSOR_IDENTIFIER	
PROCESSOR_REVISION	

4. OPTIONAL: If a printer is available in your classroom, print the file contents.

5. Close the **Computer Management** or **System Information** console.

Lab 3: Displaying Network and I/O Settings

Objectives

After completing this lab, you will be able to:

- Display network card and protocol properties.
- Display programmable interrupt (IRQ) and memory settings.

Estimated time to complete this lab: 20 minutes

Exercise 1
Displaying Local Area Connection Properties

In this exercise, you will use the **Local Area Connection Properties** dialog box to display current system network settings, including the name and resources for the adapter card, and the protocol(s) installed.

Answers recorded in this exercise may vary from student to student.

▶ **To display Local Area Connection properties**

1. Log on to the domain as Student*x*.

2. Click **Start**, point to **Settings**, and then click **Network and Dial-up Connections**.

3. Right-click **Local Area Connection**, and then click **Properties** to display the **Local Area Connection Properties** dialog box. As an alternative, you can double-click **Network and Dial-up Connections** in Control Panel.

4. Check to see whether the **Show icon in taskbar when connected** check box is selected. Record your observation in the table below.

Item	Value
Show icon in taskbar when connected	(Yes/No)

5. Click **Configure**, and open the **Resources** tab. Record the value of each item listed in the table below.

Item	Value
Input/Output Range	
Memory Range	
Interrupt Request	

6. Return to the **Local Area Connection Properties** dialog box. Select **Internet Protocol (TCP/IP)**, and then click **Properties**. Check to see whether the option buttons listed in the table below are selected. Record your observations in the table.

Item	Value
Obtain an IP address automatically	(Yes/No)
Obtain DNS server address automatically	(Yes/No)

Exercise 2
Using Windows System Information to View Network and IRQ Information

In this exercise, you will use System Information to view configuration information for your Windows 2000 Server.

▶ **To view configuration information**

1. Log on to the domain as Student*x*.

2. Click **Start**, point to **Programs**, point to **Administrative Tools**, and then click **Computer Management**. Double-click **System Information**.

3. Open **Hardware Resources** and then open **IRQs**. Observe the list of IRQ numbers and assigned devices. Record the IRQ numbers and the devices they are assigned to in the table below.

   Answers recorded in the table will vary from student to student.

IRQ Number	Device

4. Double-click the **Internet Explorer** container. Review the contents of the various containers, and locate the values of the items listed in the table below. Record the values in the table.

Answers recorded in the table will vary from student to student.

Item	Value
Page Refresh Type	
Temporary Internet Files Folder	
Total Disk Space	
Available Disk Space	
Maximum Cache Size	
Available Cache Size	

Lab 4: Configuring TCP/IP

Objectives

After completing this lab, you will be able to:

- Manually configure TCP/IP on a computer running Windows 2000.
- Use ping to verify IP connectivity.
- Use ipconfig to view IP settings.
- (Optional) Automatically configure TCP/IP by using DHCP.

Before You Begin

Before beginning this lab, your instructor should assign each student an IP address to be used in this lab. Record your assigned IP address below.

_____ . _____ . _____ . _____

Use your assigned IP address to replace the *w.x.y.z* placeholder in this lab.

This lab assumes that the Instructor*x* computer has an IP address of 10.1.1.100. If it is different, your instructor will tell you, and you should substitute the correct address for the Instructor*x* computer, where appropriate, throughout this lab.

Estimated time to complete this lab: 20 minutes

Exercise 1
Manually Configuring TCP/IP on a Computer Running Windows 2000

In this exercise, you will manually configure TCP/IP on a computer running Windows 2000.

▶ **To manually configure TCP/IP**

1. Log on to the domain as Student*x*.
2. Click **Start**, point to **Settings**, and then click **Network and Dial-up Connections**.
3. Right-click **Local Area Connection**, and then click **Properties** to display the **Local Area Connection Properties** dialog box.
4. Select **Internet Protocol (TCP/IP)**.
5. Click **Properties** to display the **Internet Protocol (TCP/IP)** dialog box.
6. Click **Use the following IP address** to indicate that you are manually configuring your IP address, and then enter the following information.

In this box	Use
IP Address	10.1.1.100 unless instructed otherwise
Subnet Mask	255.255.0.0 unless instructed otherwise
Default Gateway	Leave blank unless instructed otherwise

7. Click **OK** twice to close the two dialog boxes.

   A **Microsoft TCP/IP** dialog box appears, displaying the following message:

   ```
   The static IP address that was just configured is already in use on
   the network.  Please reconfigure a different IP address.
   ```

   Why does this message appear? Write a brief answer below.

_____

▶ **To specify a correct address**

1. Click **Start**, point to **Settings**, and then click **Network and Dial-up Connections**.
2. Right-click **Local Area Connection**, and then click **Properties** to display the **Local Area Connection Properties** dialog box.
3. Select **Internet Protocol (TCP/IP)**, and click **Properties** to display the **Internet Protocol (TCP/IP) Properties** dialog box.

4. Enter the following information to eliminate the IP conflict.

In this box	Use
IP Address	*w.x.y.z* provided by your instructor
Subnet Mask	255.255.0.0 unless instructed otherwise
Default Gateway	Leave blank unless instructed otherwise

5. Click **OK** twice to close the two dialog boxes.

Exercise 2
Using Ping to Verify IP Connectivity

In this exercise, you will use ping to verify that the TCP/IP configuration is correct.

▶ **To test and verify that the TCP/IP configuration is correct**

1. Log on to the domain as Student*x*.

2. Start a Command Prompt. (Click **Start**, point to **Programs**, point to **Accessories**, and click **Command Prompt**.)

3. To test that IP is working and bound to your adapter, type **ping 127.0.0.1** and then press ENTER.

   This internal loop-back test should give you four replies if TCP/IP is bound to the adapter.

4. To test TCP/IP connectivity with the Instructor*x* computer, type **ping 10.1.1.100** (or an address provided by your instructor) and then press ENTER.

   Four "Reply from 10.1.1.100" messages should appear.

5. Try pinging other computers in your classroom. Recall (unless noted otherwise by your instructor) that the IP addresses in your classroom are assigned as *w.x.y.z*, where *w.x.y* is exactly the same as in your own IP address, and the remainder, *z*, is unique to each student's system.

6. To view TCP/IP parameters for your computer, type **ipconfig /all** and then press ENTER.

   The TCP/IP configuration information appears. It should look similar to the information shown in the following two tables.

Windows 2000 IP Configuration

Host name	COMPUTER1
Primary DNS Suffix	corp1.corp.com
Node type	Hybrid
IP Routing Enabled	No
WINS Proxy Enabled	No
DNS Suffix Search List	corp1.corp.com corp.com

Ethernet adapter Local Area Connection

Connection-specific DNS Suffix	
Description	3Com EtherLink XL 10/100 PCI NIC
Physical Address	0-AA-00-61-3D-BE
DHCP Enabled	No
IP Address	10.1.1.1
Subnet Mask	255.255.0.0
Default Gateway	
DNS Servers	

Exercise 3 *(optional)*
Automatically Configuring TCP/IP on a Computer Running Windows 2000

In this exercise, you will configure your computer running Windows 2000 Server to obtain its IP addressing information from a DHCP server, and then view the addressing information supplied to your computer by the DHCP server.

Note This exercise must not be attempted in the classroom or lab without explicit instructions from the instructor. A DHCP server must be configured prior to the exercise, and it must not conflict with another DHCP server on the network nor issue addresses that duplicate those already being used on the network. Incorrect implementation of a DHCP server can be seriously disruptive to a network.

▶ **To automatically configure TCP/IP by using DHCP**

1. Click **Start,** point to **Settings,** and then click **Network and Dial-up Connections**.
2. Right-click **Local Area Connection,** and then click **Properties** to display the **Local Area Connection Properties** dialog box.
3. Select **Internet Protocol (TCP/IP),** and click **Properties** to display the **Internet Protocol (TCP/IP) Properties** dialog box.
4. Click **Obtain an IP Address automatically**.
5. Click **OK** twice to close the two dialog boxes.

▶ **To verify the DHCP configuration**

1. Start a Command Prompt.
2. Type **ipconfig /all**, and then press ENTER.

   The TCP/IP configuration information appears. It should look similar to the information shown in the following two tables.

   Windows 2000 IP Configuration

Host name	COMPUTER1
Primary DNS Suffix	corp1.corp.com
Node type	Hybrid
IP Routing Enabled	No
WINS Proxy Enabled	No
DNS Suffix Search List	corp1.corp.com corp.com

Ethernet adapter Local Area Connection

Connection-specific DNS Suffix	
Description	3Com EtherLink XL 10/100 PCI NIC
Physical Address	0-AA-00-61-3D-BE
DHCP Enabled	Yes
IP Address	10.1.1.50
Subnet Mask	255.255.0.0
Default Gateway	
DHCP Server	10.1.1.100
DNS Servers	

What is the IP address that the DHCP server assigned to your computer?

_____

What is the IP address of the DHCP server?

_____

Lab 5: Documenting the Network

Objectives

After completing this lab, you will be able to:

- Document the network topology used in the classroom.

Estimated time to complete this lab: 10 minutes

Exercise 1
Documenting the Network

This is a pencil-and-paper exercise in which you will learn what network topology has been installed in your classroom. Complete the table below based on information provided to you by your instructor.

Network architecture*	
Cable type	
Connection to network adapter card**	
Terminator resistance (W ohms)	
Impedance (W ohms)	
Maximum cable segment length	
Maximum connected segments	
Maximum computers per segment	

* Network Architecture: Ethernet 10Base2, Ethernet 10Base5, Ethernet 10BaseT, Ethernet 100BaseT, Ethernet 100BaseVG, Token-Ring, ArcNet, etc.

** Connection Type: RJ45, BNC, etc.

Lab 6: Hardware Compatibility List

Objectives

After completing this lab, you will be able to:

- Access and search the Hardware Compatibility List online.
- Identify the advantages of using logo'd compatible products on a computer running Windows 2000.

Before You Begin

You will need access to the Internet.

Estimated time to complete this lab: 15 minutes

Exercise 1
Accessing the Hardware Compatibility List

In this exercise, you will access and search the Hardware Compatibility List.

▶ **To access the Hardware Compatibility List**

1. Log on to the domain as Student*x*.
2. Click **Start**, point to **Programs**, and then click **Internet Explorer**.

   The Microsoft Internet Explorer window will appear.
3. Click anywhere inside the Address bar to select the current address.
4. Enter **www.microsoft.com/hcl** and click **Go**.

   The Windows Hardware Compatibility List window will appear.

▶ **To search the Hardware Compatibility List**

1. In **Search for the following**, enter **Dell**.
2. Select **System/Server Uniprocessor** from the **In the following types** drop-down list.
3. Click **Go**.

   How many Dell uniprocessor servers are NT4(x86) logo'd?

   _____

   How many Dell uniprocessor servers are Windows 2000 logo'd?

   _____

   How many Dell uniprocessor servers are NT4(x86) compatible (not logo'd)?

   _____

4. Double-click any logo'd compatible system.

   The Hardware Compatibility List – Details window appears.

   What logo level classifications does the system meet?

   _____

5. Close the Hardware Compatibility List – Details window.
6. Double-click any non-logo'd compatible system.

   What logo level classifications does the system meet?

   _____

7. Close the Hardware Compatibility List – Details window.
8. Click **Back**.
9. Close Microsoft Internet Explorer.

Exercise 2
Understanding the Advantages of Logo'd Compatibility

In this exercise, you will identify the advantages of using logo'd compatible products on a Windows 2000 computer.

▶ **To access the Hardware Compatibility List**

1. Log on to the domain as Student*x*.
2. Click **Start**, point to **Programs**, and then click **Internet Explorer**.

    The Microsoft Internet Explorer window will appear.
3. Click anywhere inside the Address bar to select the current address.
4. Enter **www.microsoft.com/hcl** and click **Go**.

    The Windows Hardware Compatibility List window will appear.

▶ **To determine the advantages of logo'd hardware on a Windows 2000 computer**

1. Click **What's the Logo?**

    The Windows Compatible Products window will appear.

    Are logo'd products tested and certified by Microsoft?

    _____

    Are logo'd products tested to see if they'll work with other logo'd products?

    _____

    Do we have both hardware and software logo'd products?

    _____

    Have logo'd products been tested to ensure they install properly and uninstall completely?

    _____

    Will logo'd products overwrite key system components?

    _____

2. Close the **Windows Compatible Products** window.
3. Close Windows Internet Explorer.

Lab 7: Creating User Accounts

Objectives

After completing this lab, you will be able to:

- Create user accounts.
- Create home folders for user accounts.
- Set restrictions for logon hours.
- Set account restrictions.
- Test a user account.

Estimated time to complete this lab: 30 minutes

Exercise 1
Creating User Accounts

In this exercise, you will create a user account on the Corp*x* domain.

This exercise is structured so that you first create an account and then modify its properties.

Important The user accounts that you create must be unique to your domain's directory database. If the instructions given in this exercise would cause two or more students to have the same user account name, add a number to the end of each of the identical names (for example, MNguyen1 and MNguyen2).

▶ **To create a new user account**

1. Log on to the domain as Student*x*.

2. Click **Start**, and then click **Run**. In **Open**, type **mmc**. Click **OK**.

   A Microsoft Management Console window will appear.

3. On the **Console** menu, click **Add/Remove Snap-in**.

   The **Add/Remove Snap-in** dialog box appears.

4. Click **Add**.

   The **Add Standalone Snap-in** dialog box appears.

5. Select **Active Directory Users and Computers**.

6. Click **Add**.

7. Click **Close**.

8. Click **OK**.

   Notice that **Active Directory Users and Computers** now appears in your console tree.

9. On the **Console** menu, click **Save**. Save your console as C:\Active Directory Users and Computers.

10. In the console tree, open **corp*x*.corp.com**.

11. Click **Users**.

    The list of existing users and groups is displayed in the right pane.

12. Right-click **Users**, point to **New**, and then click **User**.

    The **New Object - User** dialog box appears.

13. In **First name**, enter your first name, such as Mai.

14. Leave **Initials** blank.

15. In **Last name**, enter your last name, such as Nguyen.

16. In **User logon name** enter your name in the form FLastname, where you enter your first initial and first letter of your last name in capital letters, and the remainder of the characters in lowercase letters, such as MNguyen.

17. Click **Next**.

18. Leave **Password** blank.

19. Leave **Confirm Password** blank.

20. Clear the **User Must Change Password at Next Logon** check box.

21. Select the **User Cannot Change Password** check box.

22. Select the **Password Never Expires** check box.

23. Clear the **Account Disabled** check box.

24. Click **Next**.

25. Review your summary of options selected, and then click **Finish**.

Exercise 2
Modifying User Accounts

▶   **To create a home folder**

Note Complete this procedure for each user account.

1. Log on to the domain as Student*x*.
2. Open the **Active Directory Users and Computers** console that you saved in Exercise 1.
3. In the console tree, open **corpx.corp.com**, and then click **Users**.
4. In the right pane, double-click the user account that you created in Exercise 1.
5. If necessary, open the **General** tab.
6. In **Description**, enter a short phrase to describe yourself, such as Computer Networking Major.
7. Open the **Profile** tab.
8. In **Connect**, select **Z:** so that drive Z will be used to connect to the user's home folder.
9. In **To**, type **\\Instructor*x*\users\%username%** (Instructor*x* is the name of a domain controller for the Corp*x* domain, and %username% is a special variable that will be replaced by your account's user name).

Note In the classroom setup completed by your instructor prior to class, the Users folder was created and shared on the domain controller. In an actual working situation, you would also need to create and share a folder on a volume for this procedure to work.

10. Open the **Profile** tab.
11. Click **OK** to return to the User Manager window.

▶   **To set logon hours restrictions**

Note Complete this procedure for your own account.

1. Open the **Active Directory Users and Computers** console that you created in Exercise 1. Click **Users** in the console tree. In the right pane, double-click your user account.
2. Open the **Account** tab.
3. Click **Logon Hours**.

Notice that the default is to allow the user to log on to the network 24 hours a day, 7 days a week.

4. To restrict a user's logon hours, select the appropriate block of time, and then click **Logon Denied**. To enable a user's logon hours, select the block of time and then click **Logon Permitted**.

5. Using your mouse, click on the top left corner and drag to the bottom right corner of the logon hours. Click **Logon Denied**.

6. Again using your mouse, click on the starting day and time for your class and drag to the ending time for the class. Click **Logon Permitted**. Repeat this procedure for each day and time the class meets.

7. Click **OK**.

▶ **To set the account restriction**

Note Complete this procedure for each user whose account needs to expire.

1. Open the **Active Directory Users and Computers** console that you created in Exercise 1. Click **Users** in the console tree. In the right pane, double-click your user account.

2. Open the **Account** tab.

   Notice that the default option for **Account Expires** is Never.

3. Click **End of**, and then type the date for the end of your class.

4. Click **OK**.

Exercise 3
Testing the New User Accounts

In this exercise, you see that the accounts and home directories were created, and then you test the accounts.

▶ **To determine that home folders were created**

1. On the desktop, double-click **My Network Places**. Locate **Instructor*x***, the computer name for your instructor's computer.

2. Double-click **Instructor*x*** to show the shared directories for that system.

3. Double-click **Users** to display the users' folders.

4. Open the **Active Directory Users and Computers** console that you created in Exercise 1. Click **Users** in the console tree.

5. Compare the folders in the Users folder with the list of user account names in the **Active Directory Users and Computers** console.

What are the differences?

_____

▶ **To test your user account**

1. Attempt to log on using the account you created for your name.

2. For the password, enter **PASSWORD**.

Were you able to log on successfully? Why or why not?

_____

_____

3. Attempt to log on again, using **password** as the password entry.

Were you able to log on successfully? Why or why not?

_____

_____

Lab 8: Disabling and Deleting a User Account

Objectives

After completing this lab, you will be able to:

- Disable a user account.
- Delete a user account.

Estimated time to complete this lab: 10 minutes

Exercise 1
Adding a Temporary User Account

In this exercise, you will create and then delete a user account for the Corp*x* domain. This exercise is structured so that you first create the account, then disable it, and finally delete it.

▶ **To create the new user account**

1. Log on to the domain as Student*x*.

2. Open the **Active Directory Users and Computers** console that you created in Lab 7.

3. In the console tree, open **corp*x*.corp.com**.

4. Click **Users**.

   The list of existing users and groups is displayed in the right pane.

5. Right-click **Users**, point to **New**, and then click **User**.

   The **New Object - User** dialog box appears.

6. In **First name**, enter **Temp**.

7. Leave **Initials** blank.

8. In **Last name**, enter **Account*x***, where *x* is the student number you were assigned for this class.

9. In **User logon name**, enter **Temp*x***.

10. Click **Next**.

11. In **Password**, enter **password**.

12. In **Confirm Password**, enter **password**.

13. Clear the **User Must Change Password at Next Logon** check box.

14. Select the **User Cannot Change Password** check box.

15. Select the **Password Never Expires** check box.

16. Clear the **Account Disabled** check box.

17. Click **Next**.

18. Review your summary of options selected, and then click **Finish**.

Exercise 2
Testing and then Disabling the Temporary User Account

Using the account you just added to the domain, you will first log on to the
Corp*x* domain using the account to test that it is working. Then, after logging off,
you will delete the account.

▶ **To Log on using the Temp*x* account**

1. Log off.

2. When the **Welcome to Windows** dialog box reappears, press
   CTRL+ALT+DELETE to display the **Log On to Windows** dialog box.

3. In **User name**, type **Temp*x***.

4. In **Password**, type **password**.

5. In **Log on to**, select **Corp*x***.

6. Click **OK**.

You should now be logged on as the Temp*x* user. If this does not work, repeat the
steps above or ask your instructor for help. If you are having difficulty, remember
to check the spelling of the user name. Although it is not case-sensitive, the specific characters must be typed correctly, including the hyphen included in the
name and the numerical digits at the end of the name.

▶ **To disable the temporary account**

1. Log off as Temp*x*.

2. Log on to the domain as Student*x*.

3. Open the **Active Directory Users and Computers** console that you created
   in Lab 7.

4. In the console tree, open **corp1.corp.com**.

5. Click **Users**.

   The list of existing users and groups is displayed in the right pane.

6. From the list of users, right-click **Temp*x***.

   Click **Disable Account**, and then click **OK** to confirm the action.

   A red x should be displayed on the account.

7. What happens when you log off and attempt to log on as **Temp*x***?

   _____

   _____

   _____

8. Log on to the domain again as Student*x*.

9. Open the **Active Directory Users and Computers** console that you created in Lab 7.

10. In the console tree, open **corp1.corp.com**.

11. Click **Users**.

    The list of existing users and groups is displayed in the right pane.

12. From the list of users, right-click **Temp***x*.

    Click **Enable Account**.

    A red x should be removed from the account.

13. To test the account, log off and log on as Temp*x*.

14. What happens this time when you attempt to log on as Temp*x*?

    _____

    _____

Exercise 3
Deleting the Temporary User Account

▶   **To delete the Temp*x* account**

1. Log off as Temp*x*.

2. Log on to the domain as Student*x*.

3. Open the **Active Directory Users and Computers** console that you created in Lab 7.

4. In the console tree, open **corp1.corp.com**.

5. Click **Users**.

    The list of existing users and groups is displayed in the right pane.

6. From the list of users, right-click **Temp*x***.

    Click **Delete**, and then click **Yes** to confirm the action.

7. What happens when you attempt to log on as Temp*x*?

    _____

    _____

Lab 9: Using Diagnostic Utilities

Objectives

After completing this lab, you will be able to:

- Create a real-time Performance Monitor chart.
- Record data for analysis in a Performance Monitor log file.
- Summarize performance data in a Performance Monitor report.
- Install Network Monitor Tools.
- Use Network Monitor to capture and display network traffic.

Estimated time to complete this lab: 60 minutes

Exercise 1
Creating a Real-Time Performance Monitor Chart

In this exercise, you will create a chart in Performance Monitor to display performance data in real time. Real-time charts provide a quick overview of the current
performance of your system.

▶ **To configure the chart**

1. Log on to the domain as Student*x*.

2. Click **Start**, point to **Programs**, point to **Administrative Tools**, and then
   click **Performance**. This opens the **Performance** console, which has a console tree in the left pane and a blank chart in the right pane.

3. Right-click anywhere inside the chart pane, and then click **Add Counters**.

   Notice that Processor is the default performance object.

4. In the list of counters, click **% DPC Time**, and then click **Explain**.

   Notice that a counter definition appears at the bottom of the window.

5. Click each of the counters for the **Processor** object and read the counter definition for each.

6. Click the **All counters** option button.

7. Click **Add**.

8. Click **Close**.

   A graph appears, displaying the values of the counters in real time.

▶ **To generate data and view it on the chart**

1. Click **Start**, point to **Programs**, point to **Accessories**, point to **Games**, and
   then click **Pinball**.

2. Play one ball (and *only* one ball) of pinball. (To launch a ball, hold the space
   bar down for a few seconds and then release it.)

3. Close Pinball, and observe the **Performance** console.

4. In the list of counters, click **% Processor Time**, and notice the changing
   value of **Average** in the status bar below the chart.

Tip To highlight the selected counter on the chart, press CTRL+H.

---

5. Minimize Performance Monitor.

6. Click **Start**, point to **Programs**, point to **Accessories**, point to **System Tools**,
   and then click **System Information**.

7. Minimize System Information.

8. Restore Performance Monitor.

9. Notice the activity on the chart, such as spikes.

You have now created a chart displaying real-time processor utilization. This is useful because it allows you to see how your CPU is being used at the current time. In the next exercise, you will collect and save data for future reference, which can then be turned into a graph to compare with real-time data to analyze performance.

Exercise 2
Recording Data for Analysis in a Performance Monitor Log File

In this exercise, you will use Performance Monitor to create and view a log of processor activity. Logs gather and record data to a file over a period of time. Logs are useful in predicting long-term trends or in troubleshooting short-term problems.

▶   **To create a log**

1. Open Performance Monitor if it isn't already open.

2. Right-click **Counter Logs** in the console tree, and then click **New Log Settings**.

   The **New Log Settings** dialog box appears.

3. Enter **My Performance Log**, and then click **OK**.

4. Click **Add**.

5. Click **All Counters**.

6. Click **Add**.

7. Click **Close**.

8. Change the **Interval** to **1** second.

9. Open the **Log Files** tab.

10. Under **Log file size**, click **Limit of**, and change the amount to **100** KB.

11. Open the **Schedule** tab. If you are asked about creating a folder, click **Yes**.

12. Under **Start log**, click **Manually**.

13. Under **Stop log**, click **When the 100-KB log file is full**.

14. Click **OK**.

15. Double-click **Counter Logs** in the console tree.

16. Right-click **My Performance Log**, and then click **Start**.

    The log icon changes from red to green indicating that the real-time processor activity is being collected in the log.

17. Create processor activity by playing a game of pinball. Perodically check to see if the log icon has changed to red yet.

18. Wait until the icon changes from green to red, which means the file has reached 100 KB, and then proceed with the next step.

▶   **To view log data in a chart**

1. Click **System Monitor** in the console tree.

2. Right-click anywhere in the chart, and then click **Properties**.

   The **System Monitor Properties** dialog box appears.

3. Open the **Source** tab.

4. Click **Log file**.

5. Click **Browse**. Navigate until you find the My_Performance_Log file that you recently created. Select this file, and click **Open**.

6. Click **OK** to return to Performance Monitor.

   The chart displays all the recorded counters. If your chart is blank, you may need to add counters. To add counters, right-click the chart, click **Properties**, click **All Counters**, click **Add**, and click **Close**.

The chart displays the processor counters collected in your log during the data-collection period. You will notice data displayed on the chart as well as on the status bar below the chart. The status bar displays the **Last**, **Average**, **Minimum**, **Maximum**, and **Duration** values.

Leave your chart in place so you do not have to reconfigure it when you begin Exercise 3.

Exercise 3
Summarizing Performance Data in a Performance Monitor Report

In this exercise, you will view portions of the data in a chart.

▶ **To view isolated segments of log data in a chart**

1. If your chart is still in place from Exercise 2, go to step 3 below. Otherwise start Performance Monitor and configure it as described in step 2.

2. Right-click the chart, and then click **Add counters**. Click **All counters**. Click **Add**, and click **Close**. Right-click the chart, and then click **Properties**. Click **Log file**. Click **Browse**. Navigate until you find the My_Performance_Log file that you recently created. Select this file, and click **Open**.

3. In the list of counters, click **% Processor Time**.

4. Record the value of **Average** as it appears in the status bar below the chart.

_____

5. Right-click the chart, and then click **Properties**.

6. Open the **Source** tab.

   This dialog box contains a slider that is used to adjust the portion of the chart that is shown.

7. Use the mouse to position the left edge of the slider in the middle of the bar and the right edge of the slider at the right end of the bar. Click **OK**.

   The right half of the original chart is now displayed.

8. Record the value of **Average** again.

_____

9. Repeat Steps 5 through 7, this time adjusting the slider so that the last one-quarter of the chart is displayed.

10. Record the value of **Average** again.

_____

11. Repeat Steps 5 through 7, adjusting the left and right edges of the slider as necessary until the value of **Average** for the portion of the chart displayed is greater than 40 percent.

    In your opinion, how accurate is this representation of the processor's use?

_____

12. Adjust the slider control to view the entire graph.

13. Close the **Performance** console.

Exercise 4
Installing Management and Monitoring Tools

In this exercise, you will install Management and Monitoring Tools.

▶ **To install Management and Monitoring Tools**

1. Log on to the domain as Student*x*.

2. Click **Start**, point to **Settings**, and then click **Control Panel**.

3. Double-click **Add/Remove Programs**.

4. Click **Add/Remove Windows Components**.

5. Select the **Management and Monitoring Tools** check box.

6. Click **Next**.

   Management and Monitoring Tools will be installed. (You might be asked to insert the Windows 2000 CD.)

7. Click **Finish**.

8. Click **Close**.

9. Close Control Panel.

Exercise 5
Capturing Data with Network Monitor

In this exercise, you will use Network Monitor to capture and display network traffic.

▶ **To set a trigger**

1. Log on to the domain as Student*x*.
2. Click **Start**, point to **Programs**, point to **Administrative Tools**, and then click **Network Monitor**.
3. You might have to click **OK** to acknowledge a message box.
4. The Select a network window might appear. If it does, click **OK** to select the local network for monitoring.

   The Microsoft Network Monitor window appears.
5. Maximize the Microsoft Network Monitor window.
6. Maximize the Capture window within the Microsoft Network Monitor window.
7. On the **Capture** menu, click **Trigger**.

   The **Capture Trigger** dialog box appears.
8. Under **Trigger on**, click **Buffer Space**.
9. Under **Buffer Space**, click **50%**.
10. Under **Trigger Action**, click **Stop Capture**.
11. Click **OK**.

▶ **To capture network data and generate network traffic**

1. On the **Capture** menu, click **Start**.
2. Click **Start**, and then click **Run**.
3. In **Open**, type **\\Instructor*x*** and then click **OK**.

   A list of resources on Instructor*x* appears.
4. In the Instructor*x* window, double-click **NTSrv**.

▶ **To view network data statistics**

1. Switch to Network Monitor.
2. On the **Capture** menu, click **Stop** (unless data collection has already stopped).
3. On the **Capture** menu, click **Display Captured Data**.
4. Scroll through the list of captured frames. You should see your own computer name (Computer*x*) and Instructor*x*. You may also see other computer names if those computers were communicating with your server during the capture.
5. Close Network Monitor.

Lab 10: Sharing Folders

Objectives

After completing this lab, you will be able to:

- Share a folder.
- Assign shared folder permissions to users and groups.
- Connect to a shared folder.
- Stop sharing a folder.

Estimated time to complete this lab: 30 minutes

Exercise 1
Sharing Folders

In this exercise, you will share folders and assign permissions.

▶ **To share a folder**

1. Log on to the domain as Student*x*, and start Windows Explorer.

2. Create a folder named **Public** at the root directory level of drive C.

3. Right-click the newly created **Public** folder, and then click **Properties**.

4. Open the **Sharing** tab.

Tip When you right-click the **Public** folder, notice that the **Sharing** command appears on the shortcut menu. If you click **Sharing** on this menu, you will switch directly to the **Sharing** tab of the **Public Properties** dialog box.

---

5. Click **Share this folder**.

   Notice that the **Share Name** defaults to the name of the folder.

6. In **Comment**, type **Shared Public Folder** and then click **OK**.

   In Windows Explorer, what appears on the **Public** folder, indicating that it is shared?

Exercise 2
Assigning Shared Folder Permissions

In this exercise, you will determine the current permissions, remove permissions, and add permissions for existing global user groups.

▶ **To determine the current permissions for the Public shared folder**

1. Log on to the domain as Studentx.
2. In Windows Explorer, right-click the **Public** folder, and then click **Sharing**.
   The **Public Properties** dialog box appears.
3. Click **Permissions**.
   The **Permissions for Public** dialog box appears.
   What are the default permissions for the **Public** shared folder?

   _____

▶ **To remove permissions for a group**

- In the **Permissions for Public** dialog box, in **Names**, make sure **Everyone** is selected, and then click **Remove**.

▶ **To assign Full Control permission to the Domain Admins group**

1. In the **Permissions for Public** dialog box, click **Add**.
   The **Select Users, Computers, or Groups** dialog box appears.
   What domain name appears in the **Look in** box?

   _____

2. In **Names**, click **Domain Admins**.
3. Click **Add**.
4. Click **OK**.
   The **Permissions for Public** dialog box appears.
5. Under **Permissions**, select the **Allow Full Control** check box.

▶ **To assign Read permission to the Domain Users group**

1. In the **Permissions for Public** dialog box, click **Add**.
   The **Select Users, Computers, or Groups** dialog box appears.
2. In **Names**, click **Domain Users**, and then click **Add**.
3. Click **OK**.
   The **Permissions for Public** dialog box appears.
4. Under **Permissions**, select the **Allow Read** check box. Make sure all the other check boxes are cleared.

Exercise 3
Connecting to a Shared Folder

In this exercise, you will use two methods to connect to a shared folder. You will then disconnect a network drive.

▶ **To connect to a shared folder using the Run command**

1. Log on to the domain as Student*x*.
2. Click **Start**, and then click **Run**.
3. In **Open**, type **\\Instructor*x*** and then click **OK**.

   The Instructor*x* window appears.

   Notice that only the folders that are shared appear to network users.
4. Close the Instructor*x* window.

▶ **To connect to a shared folder using Map Network Drive**

1. On the desktop, right-click **My Network Places**, and then click **Map Network Drive**.
2. In **Drive**, click **P**.
3. In **Folder**, type **\\Instructor*x*\Public**.
4. Clear the **Reconnect at logon** check box, and then click **Finish**.
5. Close the **Public on 'Instructor*x*'** window.
6. Start Windows Explorer and view the drives under **My Computer**.

   Notice that the directory has been added as **Public on 'Instructor*x*'**.

   What drive letter was assigned to the mapped **\\Instructor*x*\Public** directory?

   _____

▶ **To disconnect a network drive using Windows Explorer**

1. In Windows Explorer, right-click the drive assigned to **\\Instructor*x*\Public**, and then click **Disconnect**.

   The drive is removed from the left pane of Windows Explorer.
2. Exit Windows Explorer and log off.

Exercise 4
Stop Sharing a Folder

In this exercise, you will stop sharing a shared folder.

▶ **To stop sharing a folder**

1. Log on to the domain as Student*x*.
2. Start Windows Explorer.
3. Locate and right-click the **Public** folder, and then click **Sharing**.

   The **Sharing** tab of the **Public Properties** dialog box appears.
4. Click **Do not share this folder**, and then click **OK**.

   Notice that the hand no longer appears on the **Public** folder.

Lab 11: Locating Internet Resources

Objectives

After completing this lab, you will be able to:

- Locate Microsoft Support online.
- Use ftp to access and retrieve a file online.
- Locate Microsoft TechNet online.

Estimated time to complete this lab: 30 minutes

Exercise 1
Locating Microsoft Support Online

In this exercise, you will use the Internet to access Microsoft Support online.

▶   **To locate Microsoft Support online**

1. Log on as directed by your instructor, and start Microsoft Internet Explorer.

Note To use the Internet, your system's IP address must be correct for network access through the Internet, you must have a gateway IP address, and the DNS entry must be completed. Because these addresses are unique to each location, the specific information required and the procedure for completing your TCP/IP configuration will be given to you by your instructor.

---

2. In the address bar, type the URL **http://support.microsoft.com**, and then press ENTER.
3. In **My search is about**, select the product **Windows NT Server**.
4. In **My question is**, type **DNS**.
5. Click **Go**.
6. When the system responds with a list of articles, browse the articles. Select one of interest to you and click that article to display its contents.
7. Return to the Knowledge Base Search page, and in **My Question Is**, type **How to troubleshoot basic TCP/IP problems**.
8. In **I want to search by**, click **Asking a question using a free-text query**.
9. Click **Go**.
10. When the system responds with a list of articles, browse the articles. Select one of interest to you and click that article to display its contents.
11. Return to the Knowledge Base Search page to enter other searches, or to search for articles suggested by your instructor.
12. If a printer is available on your network, print the results of one of your searches.
13. Return to the Knowledge Base Search page to enter other searches, or to search for articles suggested by your instructor.

Exercise 2
Using ftp to Retrieve a File

In this exercise, you will access Microsoft's ftp site, search for an appropriate file, and download it to your system.

▶ **To attach to Microsoft's ftp site via Internet Explorer**

1. In Windows Internet Explorer's address bar, type **ftp://ftp.microsoft.com**, and then press ENTER.

   The FTP root at ftp.microsoft.com window appears.

2. Click **dirmap.htm** or **dirmap.txt** (the first is a hypertext file, the second a text file) and read the instructions to guide you in using the ftp site. The dirmap.htm file contains links to subdirectories; if you use the text file, you will have to return to the initial page to click subdirectories.

3. Click **Windows NT** under the **BUSSYS** root directory.

4. Click **readme.txt** to learn about Windows NT files available on this site.

5. Return to the root directory of the ftp site.

6. Click **bussys**, then **WinNT**, and then **Papers** to reach the site *ftp:// ftp.microsoft.com/bussys/winnt/winnt-docs/papers*.

7. Click **readme.txt** to learn which files are in this directory.

8. Click **tcpipimp2.doc** to retrieve a document explaining the implementation of TCP/IP in Windows NT.

9. Read the file, or close it and read the file at a later time. You may also print the file and/or copy it to a floppy disk to read later.

Exercise 3
Connecting to TechNet

In this exercise, you connect to the Microsoft TechNet Web pages to learn about this subscription support service.

▶ **To connect to TechNet via the Internet**

1. In Windows Internet Explorer's address bar, type the URL **http:// www.microsoft.com/technet**, and then press ENTER.

2. After reading the TechNet page, click **TechNet CD Online** in the navigation bar at the top of the TechNet window.

3. Click **What's New** on the right side of the window.

4. Browse the page, choosing some of the options.

5. Optionally, and if a printer is available through the network, print an article from TechNet.

6. Close Internet Explorer when you have finished browsing the TechNet page.

Lab 12: Security

Objectives

After completing this lab, you will be able to:

- Access and review local security policies.
- Modify local security settings.

Estimated time to complete this lab: 15 minutes

Exercise 1
Accessing and Reviewing Local Security Settings

In this exercise, you will access and review local security on a computer running Windows 2000.

▶ **To access local security settings**

1. Log on to the domain as Student*x*.

2. Click **Start**, point to **Programs**, point to **Administrative Tools**, and then click **Local Security Policy**.

   The **Security Settings** console will appear.

   What are the four policy folders in the **Security Settings** container?

   _____

   _____

   _____

   _____

3. If necessary, double-click the **Account Policies** folder to view its subfolders.

   What are the two subfolders in the **Account Policies** folder?

   _____

   _____

4. If necessary, double-click the **Local Policies** folder to view its subfolders.

   What are the three subfolders in the **Local Policies** folder?

   _____

   _____

   _____

5. If necessary, double-click the **Public Key Policies** folder to view its subfolders.

   What are the subfolders in the **Public Key Policies** folder?

   _____

6. Click the **Audit Policy** folder located in the **Local Policies** folder.

   Current local audit policies will be displayed in the right panel.

   What is currently being audited?

   _____

7. Click the **User Rights Assignment** folder located in the **Local Policies** folder. Current user rights assignment policies will be displayed in the right panel. Who has the authority to force shutdown from a remote system?

_____

Who has the authority to log on locally?

_____

Who has the authority to shut down the system?

_____

8. Click the **Security Options** folder located in the **Local Policies** folder. Current security options policies will be displayed in the right panel. Who is allowed to eject removable NTFS media?

_____

Is it possible to disable the CTRL+ALT+DEL requirement for logon?

_____

How many days before a password expires will the user be prompted to change that password?

_____

Exercise 2
Modifying Local Security Settings

In this exercise, you will modify a local security setting so that the **Log on to Windows** dialog box does not display the previously entered user name.

▶ **To modify the local security policy**

1. Log on to the domain as Student*x*.

2. Click **Start**, point to **Programs**, point to **Administrative Tools**, and then click **Local Security Policy**.

   The **Security Settings** console will appear.

3. Click the **Security Options** folder located in the **Local Policies** folder.

   Current security options policies will be displayed in the right panel.

4. Double-click **Do not display last user name in logon screen**.

   The **Local Security Policy Setting** dialog box will appear.

5. Click **Enable**.

6. Click **OK**.

7. Log off.

8. Log on to the computer again.

   When the **Logon to Windows** dialog box appears, note that the **User name** box is blank.

Lab 13: Event Viewer

Objectives

After completing this lab, you will be able to:

- Access and read events from various event logs.
- Filter event logs and find events.

Estimated time to complete this lab: 10 minutes

Exercise 1
Accessing and Reading Event Logs

In this exercise, you will access and read events from various event logs.

▶ **To access and read event logs**

1. Log on to the domain as Student*x*.

2. Click **Start**, point to **Programs**, point to **Administrative Tools**, and then click **Event Viewer**.

   The **Event Viewer** console will appear.

   What logs appear in the console tree?

   _____

   _____

   _____

3. In the console tree, click **Application Log**.

   Application log events will be displayed in the right pane.

   What are the column headings for the application log?

   _____

   _____

   _____

4. In the console tree, click **System Log**.

   Are the column headings the same as in the application log?

   _____

5. In the console tree, right-click **System Log**, and then click **Help**.

   The Microsoft Management Console window will display the Event Viewer help file.

6. In the contents tree, double-click **Event Viewer**, double-click **Concepts**, and double-click **Event Viewer Overview**.

   The Event Viewer overview topic is displayed in the right pane.

7. Click **Application log**.

   Give an example of an application log.

   _____

8. Click **System log**.

   Give an example of a system log.

   _____

9. Click **Security log**.

Give an example of a security log.

_____

10. Close the Microsoft Management Console window.

11. In the console tree of the **Event Viewer** console, click **System Log**.

12. In the right pane, double-click the first event in the list.

What Type of event is this?

_____

What is the Event ID?

_____

What is the Source of this event?

_____

13. Click **OK**.

Exercise 2
Filtering Event Logs and Finding Events

In this exercise you will filter an event log and find an event with a given Event ID.

▶ **To filter an event log**

1. Log on to the domain as Student*x*.

2. Click **Start**, point to **Programs**, point to **Administrative Tools**, and then click **Event Viewer**.

   The **Event Viewer** console will appear.

3. In the console tree, click **System Log**.

4. On the **View** menu, click **Filter**.

   The **System Log Properties** dialog box will appear with the **Filter** tab opened.

5. In **Event types**, clear all the check boxes except for the **Warning** check box and the **Error** check box.

6. Click **OK**.

7. On the **View** menu, click **Oldest First**.

   What changes?

   _____

8. On the **View** menu, change the order back to **Newest First**.

9. On the **View** menu, click **All Records**.

   What changes?

   _____

▶ **To find an event log with a given Event ID**

1. In the console tree, click **System Log**.

2. On the **View** menu, click **Find**.

   The **Find in local System Log** dialog box appears.

3. In **Event ID**, type **6005**.

4. Click **Find Next**.

   The next log entry with Event ID 6005 will be highlighted.

5. Double-click the highlighted log entry.

   The log entry is displayed.

   What is the description of Event ID 6005?

   _____

Lab 14: Disk Defragmenter

Objectives

After completing this lab, you will be able to:

- Use Disk Defragmenter Help and explain basic concepts involving disk volumes and disk fragmentation.
- Determine if a disk needs to be defragmented.
- Defragment a disk.

Estimated time to complete this lab: 30 minutes

Exercise 1
Using Disk Defragmenter Help and Explaining Fragmentation

In this exercise, you will use Disk Defragmenter Help, and you will explain some basic concepts involving disk volumes and disk fragmentation.

▶   **To access Disk Defragmenter Help**

1. Log on to the domain as Student*x*.

2. Click **Start**, point to **Programs**, point to **Accessories**, point to **System Tools**, and then click **Disk Defragmenter**.

    The Disk Defragmenter window will appear.

3. On the **Action** menu, click **Help**.

    The Microsoft Management Console window will appear. The left pane will display a contents tree that includes **Disk Defragmenter**.

4. In the contents tree, double-click **Disk Defragmenter**, double-click **Concepts**, and double-click **Disk Defragmenter overview**.

    The Disk Defragmenter overview topic will appear in the right pane.

5. Click the **fragmented** hyperlink.

    What does *fragmented* mean?

    _____

    _____

    _____

    _____

6. Close the definition window by clicking anywhere.

7. Click the **volumes** hyperlink.

    What does *volume* mean?

    _____

    _____

    _____

    _____

8. Close the definition window by clicking anywhere.

9. Read the Disk Defragmenter overview topic.

    Briefly explain what Disk Defragmenter does.

    _____

    _____

    _____

    _____

What file systems can Disk Defragmenter work on?

_____

10. In the contents tree, find and double-click **How often to defragment a volume**.

    How often should you defragment a volume?

    _____

    _____

11. Close the Microsoft Management Console window.

Exercise 2
Determining if a Disk Needs to be Defragmented

In this exercise, you will determine if a disk needs to be defragmented.

▶ **To access Disk Defragmenter**

1. Log on to the domain as Student*x*.

2. Click **Start**, point to **Programs**, point to **Accessories**, point to **System Tools**, and then click **Disk Defragmenter**.

   The Disk Defragmenter window will appear.

   What file systems are installed on your computer?

   _____

   What are the capacity, free space, and percent free space for each disk?

   _____

   _____

▶ **To determine if defragmentation is required**

1. On the **Action** menu, click **Analyze**.

   When the analysis is complete, the **Analysis Complete** dialog box will appear.

   Does this disk need to be defragmented?

   _____

2. Click **View Report**.

   What are the values of **Total fragmentation, File fragmentation**, and **Free space fragmentation**?

   _____

   _____

3. Click **Close**.

4. Close the Disk Defragmenter window.

Exercise 3
Defragmenting a Disk

In this exercise you will defragment a disk.

▶   **To defragment a disk**

1. Log on to the domain as Student*x*.

2. Click **Start**, point to **Programs**, point to **Accessories**, point to **System Tools**, and then click **Disk Defragmenter**.

   The Disk Defragmenter window will appear.

3. Click **Defragment**.

   What does the **Defragmentation display** show?

   _____

   Where is the indicator that shows how much of the defragmentation process has completed?

   _____

   When the defragmentation process is complete, which color does NOT show in the **Defragmentation display**?

   _____

4. Click **Stop.**

5. Close the Disk Defragmenter window.

Scenario A: Impact of a New Full-time Employee

Objectives

After completing this lab, you will be able to:

■ Articulate the operational impact of a new employee.

Scenario

A new full-time employee, Mark Hanson, has been hired. You are responsible for ensuring he has access to resources he will need to do his job and yet cannot access information he is not authorized to see.

1. What tool is used to create a user name and password for Mark?

   _____

2. List the steps you would take to create his user account.

   _____

   _____

   _____

   _____

   _____

3. Explain how you would ensure Mark only has access to resources required for his job and is denied access to other resources. (Hint: Is it feasible to assign each person individual access rights to every resource, or can access be granted based on something that might work for more than one person at a time?)

   _____

   _____

   _____

   _____

   _____

Scenario B: Impact of a Temporary Employee

Objectives

After completing this lab, you will be able to:

- Articulate the operational impact of a temporary employee.

Scenario

A new temporary employee, Sherri Hart, has been hired. Human Resources has informed you of her beginning and ending dates of employment. The Security Officer has asked you how you can be certain that Sherri's account cannot be utilized the day after her temporary employment contract expires.

1. How will you be sure that Sherri's account cannot be used after the termination date?

   _____

   _____

   _____

   _____

2. Why would disabling an account for a temporary employee be better than deleting it?

   _____

   _____

   _____

   _____

   _____

Scenario C: Remote Help Desk

Objectives

After completing this lab, you will be able to:

- Demonstrate how a help desk can take advantage of system information on remote computers.

Scenario

You are working at the internal help desk for your company when someone calls in for help. To get system configuration information, you ask for a copy of the system information and event logs. It soon becomes clear that the customer has not kept a log and doesn't even understand your question.

1. What administrative tool will you use to connect to the customer's computer?

_____

2. What information about the customer's computer will you need before you can connect to it?

_____

3. Where can the customer find the name of their computer? (Hint: Network identification of the full computer name.)

_____

_____

4. How would you identify the file system on the customer's C: drive and the amount of available free space (disk space not RAM)?

_____

_____

_____

Scenario D: Monitoring for Unauthorized Logons

Objectives

After completing this lab, you will be able to:

- Monitor a network for unauthorized logon attempts.

Scenario

Since your network was recently attached to the Internet, your boss is concerned about hackers. He asks you to monitor all logon attempts to the network.

1. Which security settings specify that every failed logon attempt be recorded in the event log?

   _____

   _____

2. You decide that your event logs are getting too many entries from authorized users failing to enter their passwords correctly. You decide to test if the Performance Logs and Alerts snap-in can measure the number of logon attemts and failures. Will Performance Logs and Alerts track the total number of logon attempts and the logon failures?

   _____

3. What objects and counters would you want to track with Performance Logs and Alerts?

   _____

   _____

4. If Permance Logs and Alerts does track logons, what pattern of activity might indicate that a hacker is attempting to break into your system?

   _____

   _____

   _____